Full STEAM Ahead!

Ben Gwozdz

Full STEAM Ahead!

How to Use Your
Space
Time
Energy
And
Money

To create a simpler,
well-balanced life

By Bev Gwozdz

An Extra Hand Publishing,
Souderton, Pa

This book is dedicated
to all my dear clients
and to everyone
who has ever come
to hear me speak.
You have opened your hearts to me,
shared your frustrations and challenges,
questions and concerns
guilt and confusion,
and have taught me
everything I know today.

ભ

I sincerely thank you for
all the learning opportunities
you have given me.

Contents

Introduction

For the last six years, I have been shuffling through people's underwear drawers, crawling around in their closets, looking under their beds, and handling their most confidential documents. No, I am not a private detective (although I think I'd be a pretty good one). I am a professional organizer.

What I have seen over and over again is that in our stressful busy lives, we often act like mountain climbers on a steep cliff - we don't dare LOOK DOWN for fear of becoming (even more) overwhelmed by all the things that we have to deal with. Mortgage payments, a no-future job, noisy neighbors, a weed infested lawn, a gas-guzzling car, piles of papers, broken gadgets, dusty skis, an empty aquarium are crying for our attention and we end up calling for help.

It's easy to get stuck with all this unfinished business – overwhelmed to the point of paralysis - when we feel our resources are already pushed to the limit. But there are many simple skills we can learn that will help us get unstuck such as how to develop our focus, how to break a job into small steps, and how to create and use a simple checklist. These skills can be applied to your own personal challenges and will help you create a simpler low-stress life.

In this book, you will find tips and tools for using your STEAM resources - Space, Time, Energy and Money – to help you manage and balance your life.

I've heard people say that houseplants thrive when you talk to them. Though this may seem so, I feel the key to their good health is **paying attention** to them. Are the leaves nice and green? Is the soil too moist? Is there enough sunlight? When you get up close enough to a plant to speak to it, then you are close enough to carefully observe it and will know if it needs some additional care.

When you think about it, every aspect of our lives would benefit if we paid better attention - our health, our relationships, our jobs, our spending. In this book, I have included exercises that will help you learn how to pay attention to the areas that matter in your life.

Full STEAM Ahead is for you if...
- You feel overwhelmed by the stuff in your life
- You are constantly misplacing things
- You are often late for work, for bills, for dates
- In spite of having more stuff than ever, you feel depleted
- You can't see a light at the end of your tunnel
- You are racing like mad, but running out of steam

Creating a simpler life for yourself will require both *skill* and *will*, that is a combination of inspiration and practical techniques which you will find throughout this book. Feel free to browse through the tips, tools and exercises. Then take your time to **do the exercises** in any order. Simply reading the text, however, will not give you the insight and results that the simple **hands-on exercises** will!

Look around you – at your home, your family life, and your activities, listen to your head and heart, and **dare to believe** that taking charge of your STEAM resources will help give you the ability to create a simpler, well-balanced life.

These are some of the ways you will benefit from this book:

You will learn how to maximize **SPACE** by
- Eliminating clutter
- Arranging items for optimal use
- Creating activity centers

You will learn how to save **TIME** by
- Tackling procrastination
- Combining complementary activities
- Delegating household chores

You will learn how to conserve your **ENERGY** by
- Developing better focus
- Learning to motivate yourself
- Nurturing relationships

You will learn how to save **MONEY** by
- Creating a budget that works for you
- Planning meals and shopping wisely
- Doing more for yourself

Maybe today is finally the day to stand up and take action to simplify and balance your life so that it meets your needs. It's your decision. If you **choose to try**, a wonderful experience awaits you.

"Every action begins with the decision to try."

-anon

Chapter One - Getting Started

> "The starting point of all achievement is desire"
> - Napoleon Hill

As a professional organizer, one of my main goals is to help each of my clients achieve a "user-friendly" lifestyle.

What does that mean?

Merriam Webster defines "user-friendly" as "easy to learn, use, understand or deal with." I believe that when your life is organized according to your particular needs and values, it will be simple and easy for you to deal with, and will therefore be user-friendly.

One of my first clients was a woman in her early 80's who was a Taurus, and she was very set in her ways. Her biggest complaint was that she as constantly misplacing things, especially jewelry.

As I was assessing the layout of her home, I noticed random pieces of jewelry on a buffet in the dining room, and I quickly figured out why. She would typically pass through the dining room as she entered and left the house. Upon entering, she would pull off her jewelry, or at least some of it, and plunk it down on the buffet. She would take off the other pieces and put them anywhere – bathroom, kitchen sink, coffee table – they could end up anywhere. Since the buffet made sense to her as a place to take off her jewelry, and there was a mirror there for putting on jewelry, we decided to make the top drawer of the buffet her official jewelry spot, and I organized it all very nicely there. Keeping jewelry in the dining room was user-friendly for her unique lifestyle.

Your lifestyle should be user-friendly and UNIQUELY YOURS.

The Stressmobile's in Town

I can't. I can't. I can't. In my profession, I hear those words in every cry for help I receive. **"I can't..."**

- I can't keep track of unpaid bills
- I can't entertain anymore, I so ashamed of my place
- I can't find any space to store Christmas decorations
- I can't park my car in the garage
- I can't eat at the dining table, it's so covered with stuff
- I can't see how my daughter can study in this mess

These complaints all indicate one thing –

The Stressmobile is parked in your driveway!

You know you are stressed when you hear that nasty inner voice while you are tearing around the house, rummaging through your jacket pockets or plunging your hand down into the sofa cushions looking for your car keys? You are stressed when you realize that you are going to be late for work – again – because you couldn't find anything to wear. You are stressed to know you'll have to buy an overpriced tasteless sandwich for lunch because you didn't have time to pack your lunch. You are stressed when you can't find time to... can't keep up with...

When your life seems like an obstacle course of things you can't do, it's time to take action. Even spending a half-hour each day to learn ways to break the patterns of negativity and defeat in your life will reap rewards and allow you to **become the boss of your own life.** Then you can send that Stressmobile out of your life for good.

"Tension is who you think you should be. Relaxation is who you are."

~Chinese Proverb

Touching Base with Yourself

I think most people know deep down inside what they need in life. It's pretty basic – food, drink, cuddles, a cozy house, the warmth of family and friends, a creative outlet. Something to do, something to love and something to look forward to. A passion, a purpose, and hope.

When we don't have what we need in life, it's often because of our circumstances – but only for a while. If we continue to live a lifestyle that doesn't meet our needs but we don't do anything about it, then we are sabotaging our happiness.

Touching base with ourselves means taking the time to honestly look at what's wrong, and not just distract ourselves with addictive behaviors such as overeating or partying, shopping or gambling. If we are in a rut, we must focus on the issue and attack it head on, starting with small steps. For example, if you find you are eating too much fast food, you could start addressing the problem by planning your meals and making sure you eat often and well enough that you won't cave in to temptation. If you are spending too much time on the internet, you could start fixing the problem by using a timer and limiting yourself to 20 minutes a day. The solution starts with understanding what's going on, and then deciding to do something about it.

Touch base with yourself twice a day.

Just before bedtime is a good time to tidy things up, review your day, pat yourself on the back for your accomplishments, and make a list of any unfinished business that you should tackle in the morning.

First thing each morning is a good time to meditate, pray, or reach your soul in your own personal way. It's the right time to set your sails for fresh accomplishments and review your notes from the night before.

Morning and night count your blessings. Then count them again.

Focusing on what is right in your life will help give you the strength to face and correct the things that aren't quite right...yet.

The Power of Self-Speak

Hey, keep it down! Can't you see I'm trying to sleep?

In our busy lives, our waking hours are filled with thoughts - some conscious, others not. Thoughts tend to lead to feelings, and then to actions. For example, when you hear that a storm is coming, your thought is to close the windows. You feel a little uneasy, so you decide to call your kids and tell them to bring the dog inside.

That is an example of a harmless neutral thought. But many of us have a whole series of pre-recorded negative thoughts that we play to ourselves, often in bed at night when there are no distractions. These negative thoughts are often harsh, judgmental, or pessimistic, and can harm our mental state, ability to function and of course ability to sleep.

Let's say you missed the deadline for a report at work. Your negative thought might be "Here you go again, dummy!" or "My boss must think I'm a loser" which can result in a sleepless night and a weary tomorrow.

As every coach knows, mistakes happen and there's a lesson to be learned each time. So the trick is that when you screw up, take prompt action to correct the situation and learn the lesson that will keep it from happening again. When you learn to coach yourself with positive self-speak - *atta boy* or *you can do it* - it will reduce pain, stress, and worry and increase focus, energy, awareness, and confidence.

Try this exercise. Next time you feel low, tune into your feelings and see how you match up with the images below. "Nobody likes me or cares about me" (10) or "I'll never ever get a promotion."(8) Then remind yourself that *thinking*, like breathing, blinking, swallowing, and coughing, *can be automatic OR controlled*. Why not choose to think positive thoughts that can help you learn and grow?

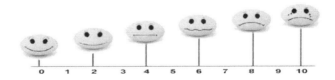

"Whether you think you can, or think you can't, you're right."
-Henry Ford

The Big Trade Off

In real life, everything we do has a price on it. There is no such thing as a free lunch. So as we decide to rebalance our lives, or use our resources in a new way, we should understand its price in terms of what we give up and what we get in return. Then decide if it is a worthwhile investment.

Here are a few examples:

What You Give Up	What You Gain	Was it Worth It?
$75	A new dress	Yes, if you will wear it more than once
2 hours	Reruns of Jeopardy	Did you need that more than a nap?
3 shelves	Storage for old craft materials	No. Now you have books on the floor!
2 Big Burger Combos per week	A gym membership	Yes. Your pants all fit nicely again!
Put $25/week into savings	$1,300/yr for vacations	Yippee!!
One hour purging junk in closet	Nice roomy space for coats and jackets	Indeed!
15 minutes to make a pre-printed grocery list for your needs	An foolproof way to buy what you need	Yes. You will save time, money, energy and space!

Now use the last four rows to record your own trade-off's.
This exercise will help you see how to create balance.

Four Legs for Balance

Three major components of our personal resources are Time, Space and Money. These often dictate where we live, the type of car we drive, if we work or not, how we spend our evenings, what hobbies we may have, and many other aspects of our lives.

But the resource that trumps them all is what I call "energy." This is the soul, passion, love, and the power of our physical being, which provides the zest, the punch, the vision and the courage not just to get through our complicated and challenging lives, but to find ways to excel and achieve. It is the fourth leg, and provides balance and strength.

This internal energy powered Anne Frank to write when she had so few physical resources. It was what gave Helen Keller the courage to face and surmount her disabilities. It is the thrust and guts that is demonstrated by great world leaders. Where does this energy come from?

A part of this energy is our physicality which is derived from good food, ample water, a decent night's rest, sufficient physical exercise. But a great amount comes from the inside – through introspection, spirituality, self-awareness, and a sense of connection through friends and family.

Humans are gregarious, which means social, liking companionship, belonging to a social group. So most humans get and maintain energy from their relationships.

When we add energy to the mix of time, space and money, it defines how we spend our free time, how we have fun, even how we decide to use our resources. As a result of maximizing our personal energy, we can better achieve a richer and better-balanced life.

> "Life is like riding a bicycle. To keep your balance you must keep moving."
> Albert Einstein

A Piece of the Puzzle

Consider each day to be
An Important Piece
of your life.

You may not be able to see
how that piece will fit into
the bigger puzzle
of your life.

But cherish this day,
and use it wisely.

It may be more important to your future
than you could ever imagine.

MAKE EACH DAY COUNT

List four things that are happening in your life today
that could impact your future.

1. _____

2. _____

3. _____

4. _____

Watch Out for That Learning Curve in the Road Ahead

Fact: the expression "No pain, no gain" was coined with muscle building in mind. Unless you work out hard enough to actually damage the muscle, your muscles won't gain strength and size.

But in fact, *No Pain No Gain* can apply to learning any new skill. How about learning to walk? Kids don't give up - they keep on tumbling, tripping, falling and getting up to try again. Remember the first time you tried to hammer in a nail? Or tried to eat with chop sticks, learn a foreign language, wind surf, sew a dress or put together a piece of furniture from a kit? Ouch! It's awkward, frustrating, embarrassing, and maybe even painful. But it's still worth it in the end, when you have mastered the new skill and it becomes a part of your life.

Between the first painful baby steps and the proud mastery of a skill, there are a couple stages. All together, from soup to nuts, the levels are called the Four Levels of Competency.

I. Unconscious incompetency. If someone asked how to care for a boa constrictor, you might say, "I haven't got a clue." You don't know how, and you don't even know what you would NEED to know to do it. You are unconscious or unaware, and (excuse me for being blunt) totally incompetent. This is where most five year olds are when it comes to balancing a check book, where most people are for settling their parents' estate. It's the ZERO level.

II. Conscious incompetence. This is when you are aware of how much you don't know. Let's say you are studying French and have learned some basic vocabulary, and then watch "Amelie" on TV. Instead of applauding yourself for how much you have learned, you see long road ahead. This is when we feel overwhelmed.

3. Conscious competence. You are quite able to do what you need to do, but it takes full concentration and focus – such as driving on an icy road, or in my case, skiing without breaking a leg.

4. Unconscious competence. Ahhhh! Now *that* feels good! This when you can do something well without even thinking – tying your shoes, riding a bike, driving a car, etc. You're on autopilot. It's become a habit.

The same type of learning curve applies to getting organized. It may require doing things that seem awkward – simply because they are outside of your comfort zone. Well, Folks, maybe your comfort zone isn't so very comfortable anymore and needs to be changed! Otherwise you wouldn't be looking at this book. So dare to try out some new approaches to how you see and use your resources.

I invite you to explore with an open heart the many quick, easy and fun organizing techniques I have compiled in this book to will help simplify your life and remove some stress. Let's get started!!!

Chapter Two - Creating a Plan that Works for You

Some planning should be included in any transition or event in our lives - expecting a baby, looking towards college, approaching retirement, getting ready for a trip.

If we don't plan, we let Fate take charge, and Fate does not know what we want, what we need, or what we aspire to.

Even if you are not the "planning type" go ahead and dare to make a plan for your day, or your week, or your future – it's free of charge. You can always change your plans later, and no one will know any better. But planning will give you a much better chance of getting where you want to go. Try it and see the results.

> "If you want to be happy, set a goal that commands your thoughts, liberates your energy, and inspires your hopes."   - Andrew Carnegie

> *"It's not so much where you are but where you are heading."*
> *-Bruce Lee*

Good Enough

"Being happy doesn't mean that everything is perfect. It means that you've decided to look beyond the imperfections."

There seems to be a great debate about **whether or not to be organized**! Some say being organized *improves efficiency*, while others claim that being organized *stifles creativity*.

Who is right?

Well, the truth is that having some structure and order is vital to the survival in our complex culture. Imagine a day without it:

Every aisle in the supermarket is marked "Whatever." There are no stop signs or traffic lights at intersections, no schedules, no alphabetization or numerical order. There are no street maps, pedestrian crosswalks or yield signs, no recipe books or reference manuals? The mind boggles.

So order is important to us, but HOW MUCH order you need depends on your particular lifestyle. A surgeon may need to be more organized than a gardener, a pilot more organized than a writer. The question is *does your current lifestyle meet your needs*? Can you easily access things that are important to you? Is your life simple enough to give you peace of mind? If not, you may be the victim of *clutter*.

Clutter Control

Is It Clutter?

Defining clutter can be tricky business. I choose to define clutter as anything that is NOT...

- *B*eautiful (Is it a pleasure to look at? Can you see it?)
- *U*seful (Do you use it for your daily activities?)
- *S*entimental (Does it bring back fond memories?)

According to John Carlos Baez in www.wordpress.com, the Inuits of North America have 49 words to describe different types of snow and ice. I don't need that much detail, but I don't consider these words as clutter, since they are useful for the Inuits.

Clutter often reflects an **unrealistic connection** with the past or the future. For example, someone may be keeping an object because it *used to* fit, **used to** work, or **used to** look nice (but doesn't anymore). Or because it *might be* useful at some undefined future time (such as *if* you lose enough weight to wear those size 10 pants again or *if* one day you buy another dog who will use the leash, bowl, crate and toys you are hanging onto). In the meanwhile, the person holds onto the object, which may in time die a slow death from exposure to dust, extreme temperatures, humidity and parasites. Sometimes...

It's better to purge and bear the pain
Than store all the junk and feel the shame.

What are two areas you should declutter? _____ and _____

Make a Plan, Set Numerical Limits, and Work Clockwise

Let's say you want to start organizing your whole house. To make that dream a reality, you'll need some strategy!

Set specific goals such as "free up dining room table" or "prepare guest room" and a plan for completion. Be realistic in choosing your target date - soon enough that you get energized – but allowing time for the unplanned events that will surely pop up. In other words, set yourself up for SUCCESS! Work in small increments, and always leave time for clean up at the end of the session!

Decide in advance the actual number of items you plan to keep, for example **two** sets of coasters, **ten** sweaters, a **dozen** candles - and get rid of the rest. Deciding quantities ahead of time will make it much easier to purge as you go.

Working clockwise around the room or area makes it easy to stay on a focused path, to see progress as you move along, and to keep track of where you left off.

Plan	Limits	Target Date
Entertainment center	Keep only top ten videos No home recorded TV shows Alphabetize CD's	Aug 20
Pantry	Check expiration dates Max: one shelf for cans Donate extras to food drive	Aug 27
Mud room closet	Keep 4 best umbrellas Keep 2 best hats each Two pairs gloves per person	Sept 1
Your area _____	Set your limits _____	Your target _____

Elimination Checklist

This is one of the first steps in getting organized. Here are several ways get rid of items that create clutter:

☑**Sell them.** A yard sale is a lot of work, but can be fun and fairly profitable. Find a consignment shop that will take your valuables. Try E-bay. Place an ad in the local newspaper if you have large items.

☑**Give them away.** Family and friends may be interested, but check with them first, and be honest about the quantity and condition of the items. You don't want to clutter their lives! Donate to charitable groups. Most donations are eligible for tax deduction, including donations to school and libraries. You can also donate to a local clothing or food drive.

☑**Home store them**. Some people use the "time capsule" approach, by removing the item from the general usage area, and storing it in a box at the back of a closet or basement. The box is labeled with its contents, and the date the box was stored. Then 6 or 12 months later, the box can be discarded without guilt and worry! Good for children's toys and books.

☑**Store them offsite**. This should be used only as a last resort, when you are sure that yours circumstances will soon change, i.e., getting a bigger house, kids will need furniture, etc. Rental storage costs mount up quickly, and once in place, people often develop an "out-of-sight, out-of mind" philosophy.

☑**Recycle or toss them**. Certain restrictions may apply for bulky items, hazardous materials (paints, thinners, aerosols, pesticides, motor oil, tires, etc). Check with your local waste management company for details. Also check the internet for local recycling events.

By the way, some people believe if you get rid of something you've had for years (such as a bright red button), ***you will develop a sudden need*** for a bright red button. This can happen. So go out and buy a new button if you need one! If you hang onto everything for that one chance in a million that you might need it, you will miss a chance to have a simple well balanced home.

One In, One Out

If Martians were in a space ship looking down at our planet, they could easily figure out how our lives get so cluttered. The little humans are always taking lots of big bags of stuff into their houses, but they only see a few little ones leaving. So where does the stuff go?

It's not rocket science. Do the math. You already have a quite full closet. At Christmas, you get a sweater from your sister, PLUS a robe from your husband, PLUS an outfit from your mother, PLUS a gift card from your boss. You use the gift card to get a pair of pants. How can that all fit in your closet when it was cramped to begin with? It's like a lobster trap that's easy to enter and hard to leave!

A good strategy is to purge what you don't need, then decide that each time a new element enters your life, you will get rid of an old item of equal size. This one-in, one-out method will help you maintain balance in all aspects of your resources - Space, Time, Energy and Money!

One In, One Out	
When this enters...	**This must go!**
A new sweater	An old shapeless sweater
A new wreath	The faded one from the back door
A new project	A chunk of TV time
Payments on the new car	Eating out every week
Christmas cookies galore	Eat low calorie snacks in New Year
Your last purchase??	*What should you let go? DO IT!*

"There is no dignity quite so impressive, and no independence quite so important, as living within your means." — Calvin Coolidge

Know Thyself

What's' your type – hare or tortoise,
night owl or early bird?

It's important for you to know
when your brain is at its peak,
and use that time for
your mentally challenging projects.

Look at the time slots below, and put a plus (+) in the slots when you are most alert and a minus (-) when you are least alert. Keep your peaks in mind when you schedule your daily activities.

Time of day (+) or (-)	Time of day (+) or (-)
6:30-8:30 am	2:30-4:30 pm
8:30-10:30 am	4:30-6:30 pm
10:30-12:30 pm	6:30-8:30 pm
12:30-2:30 pm	8:30-10:30 pm

Your best time of day for focused mental tasks: _____

Set Reasonable Deadlines

Why is it that so many people cannot find time to do their income taxes between January 31st, when most tax documents have been received, and the official deadline of April 15th? That's 73 days!

Yet these same people somehow manage to do their taxes in a 24-hour sprint between April 14th and 15th?

Why do people get that incredible burst of energy and focus? Because they feel they HAVE TO!
That is the deadline set by the IRS.

Learning to *set your own reasonable deadlines* is an important skill for establishing simplicity and balance in your life. A deadline is reasonable when it includes some wiggle room for interruptions and set-backs. Once the deadline has been set, post it in a visible location and stick to it! If it is a complex project, create mini-deadlines within so you can chart your progress and stay on track.

> **Deadlines are great motivators, but waiting till the last minute can be dangerous and stressful.**

Set a reasonable deadline for each project you are working on:

Project _____ Deadline: _____

Project _____ Deadline: _____

Project _____ Deadline: _____

Chapter Three - Owning Your Space

Your space is...

Your environment

Your territory
Your nest
Your place
Your turf
Your shelter
YOUR NOOK
Your castle
Your cave

Whatever you call it,
Wherever you roam
There's just no place
Like **Home Sweet Home**

Your space is where you live, sleep, eat, work and play, where you create meals and interact with the people you are closest to in your life. It is where you plan and laugh and let your hair down. It is where you go to recharge your internal batteries so you can face life's challenges.

Large or small, rich or simple, town or country, your **space is vital to the quality of your life**, and deserves your time, energy and attention to make it **just right for you**.

Seeing Is Believing

Take a moment for this quick exercise. Note your start time, then count all the objects on this page. How many bells, clocks, stars, etc. do you see? Note your stop time. How long did it take to count them?

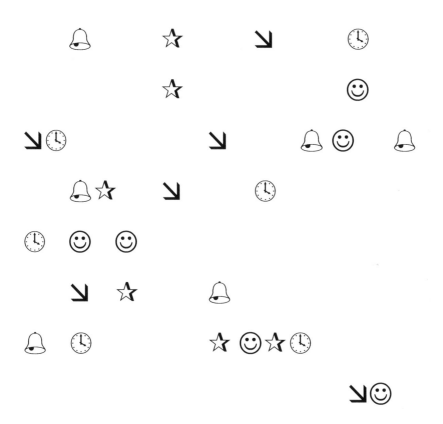

Now turn the page...

Now count the objects on this page. How many of each shape? How long did it take you to count them this time?

You have just experienced one of the basic principles of organizing -
Keep Similar Items Together.
Grouping similar items allows you to easily see how many you have, what type they are, and to save space by stacking or nestling them.

Now **where** should you group and store them? Here are some ideas...

Maximize Use of "Prime Space"

"Prime space" is any area, such as a drawer or a shelf, that you can reach without bending or stretching. It's your physical comfort zone!

It's the "front and center" where you should keep items you use most often. In your kitchen, the most prime space you have is your countertop. Use it wisely!

- Make sure you keep your countertop clear as it is your main work space for food preparation and serving.

- Consider **The Frequency Factor**. Keep only things you use on a regular basis on your countertop.

- If you have fresh juice, coffee, and toast every morning, then your toaster, coffee maker, and juicer should be on the countertop for easy access.

- Use your easy-to-reach prime cabinets for everyday dishes, glassware, and most common staple food products.

- Less frequently used items such as fondue pots, bread makers, blenders, canisters, and waffle irons can be kept in harder to reach places such as high or low shelves or even in another room.

- If you use paper plates and cups only once a year, buy them when you need them.

List here what you *need* to keep handy on your kitchen counter:

1._____ 2._____ 3._____ 4._____

List here items you can place in an out-of-the-way place:

1._____ 2._____ 3._____ 4._____

Gain Cupboard, Cabinet, Fridge and Freezer Space

You can gain valuable space – and save yourself some time - by keeping small items such as frozen veggies, spice packets and cereal bars in **small bins or baskets** that you can easily grab and rummage through you need them.

To gain even more space, remove dried foods (crackers, cereal, rice, etc.) from their boxes, fold over and clip the **inner liner bags**, and recycle the boxes. Storing things in the bags allows you to **see at a glance** how much is there, while a box sitting on a shelf doesn't tell you when it's almost empty! If needed, cut the name, cooking directions, or nutritional information from the box before you throw it away, and **clip it onto the bag for reference**.

If you find you often have **small portions of cereal** left over, mix them together and keep them in a see-through canister. The family is more likely to use this tasty fun combination if it is visible and accessible.

Lastly, if you tend to buy family size containers of flour, pickles, ketchup, etc., then find you have them forever, trade off the few cents you saved for a smaller size that **keep its freshness** and **saves you valuable space**.

> *Check off the categories below as you streamline each category in your cabinets:*
> 1. Cereal ☐   2. Crackers ☐   3. Cookies ☐   4. Pasta ☐
> 5. Tea bags ☐   6. Rice ☐   7. Grains ☐   8. Other ☐

What are some overstocked items you have that you can donate to the local food pantry?

_____

Store things near the Point of Use

One tip for good management of space is to keep things near the place where you will actually use them.

Keep your dishes near the dishwasher, pans near the stove, spare bed linens in each bedroom, mugs near the coffee maker, cat food near the cat's dish, glass cleaner, paper towels and t-paper in each bathroom, and cooking utensils near the stove.

Keys can be kept on a hook near the door, remote controls in a basket on the coffee table, umbrellas, hats scarves and gloves in personal baskets in the coat closet or mud room, and table linens in the dining room.

Hang the paint can opener on a nail above the paint. Keep special light bulbs in the room in which they'll be used.

Be sure to keep a small first aid kit containing Band-Aids, antiseptic and ointment in the kitchen, where most burns and cuts occur.

Save yourself a few steps several times each day!

Your Terribly Important, Versatile Kitchen Table

If the kitchen is the epicenter of your home, the **kitchen table is its heart**. Temptingly available for use as a craft center, mail room, and dumping ground, the kitchen table can often disappear under thick layers of miscellany.

One solution to the problem of clutter on the kitchen table or in any shared space is to assign **one sturdy basket** with handle to each family member for his/her personal belongings.

Together with the family, decide on a couple of *reasonable* **five-minute time slots each day** for each member to gather personal stuff into his basket to put away when it is convenient. Before meals and before bedtime are logical times that work for most families.

> *The basket strategy works well throughout the house for corralling electronic devices, recycling, odd bits of clothing, papers, and so on and helps avoid losing things!*
>
>

When will you and your family clear off the table? _____

Where can you use baskets in your home/office to help maintain order?

1._____ 2. _____ 3. _____

Zoom Out

What are we looking at? Forest? Trees?

Sometimes we get so caught up in our feelings that we lose sight of the big picture.

For example, let's say you have decided to clear out the guest bedroom which has become a sort of giant walk-in storage closet, if you can manage to walk in!

You are dismayed and flooded with guilt by the piles of stuff in there – out-of-season clothing, suitcases akimbo, rolls of gift wrap, a broken lamp, boxes and bins of random stuff.

If you allow yourself to focus on the overwhelming mess of it all, you'll probably give up without even trying.

This is the perfect time to zoom out.

See it for what it is - a messy room with no room for guests! But you are the **Boss of Your Stuff**! All you need to do is grab some empty boxes and a trash can, clear a quick path so you can reach the bed, set your timer, and start sorting – things to give away in one box, anything that belongs in another room in the second box, stuff to throw away in the trash can, and things that belong in this room in a tidy pile.

Don't get lost in the details! Don't stop or leave the room till the timer goes off, then pat yourself on the back!

Feeling good about your accomplishment will draw you back to finish the job because...

SUCCESS IS THE GREATEST MOTIVATOR!

Zoom In

We just zoomed out. Now we zoom in. Isn't that a contradiction?

Yes and no. Sometimes the only way we can move forward is by getting into the **nitty gritty details**.

- If you are trying to cut back on your spending, you may need to look at each grocery store receipt to see where your dimes and dollars are going.
- Trying to lose weight? Read the calorie content on each packaging label.
- Trying to set up a sewing center? It will mean dealing with buttons and snaps, needles and pins.

> Sometimes **it's the little things**
> we need to focus on
> to get us to our goal.

It's like the difference between baking a cake and baking a cupcake. The smaller the item, the more precise we need to be! For many of us, each single dollar, calorie, or square foot can have tremendous importance in our lives.

What areas of your life would be improved if you zoomed in?

1. _____

2. _____

3. _____

Think Inside the (Labeled) Box

Keep Similar Items Together, and store them where they make the most sense.

Use Containers to protect stored items, keep them together, and make things neat. You can also gain space by stacking containers of similar sizes and shapes.

Label the Containers so you know what's in them.

Here are some examples:

You can keep **wrapping paper**, ribbons, bows, and gift bags in a clear plastic bin under a spare bed.

You can assign a labeled **basket** for each family member to corral hats, gloves, scarves, umbrellas and keep the basket on a shelf in the entryway to your house.

You can use a large clear plastic bin on your closet shelf for holding **sweaters** that might otherwise tumble onto the floor.

Consider using containers you might already have on hand (boxes, bins, baskets, suitcases and such) before buying more!

Store tote bags or overnighters inside larger **suitcases**, and attach to the handle a visible tag listing the contents.

Make a **master list** to record what you keep in each storage area of your house, such as Christmas decorations under basement stairs, luggage in attic, camping supplies in the garage, past tax returns under the guest bed, etc.

Keep the list in your computer or a print out in a file in your office so you can "find things" without even getting out of your chair!

In how many rooms of your house do you store things? _____

*Do you need to make a master storage list?*_____

Create Activity Centers

A great way to use space and make your home user-friendly is to create activity centers. An activity center area can be an entire room, a section of a room, or even just a piece of furniture such as a desk, a table, or a special chair. Each area should be comfortable and equipped with the necessary tools or accessories for the activity. Here are some examples of activity centers for your home:

Reading Area. I have worked with many clients who collect articles and magazines, print outs and hand outs to read some day, but don't have an assigned place for reading! All you need is a comfortable seat with adequate lighting and a surface to put a beverage, note pad and pen on.

Craft Area. The dining room table is a great place to work on crafts. Keep supplies in a handy basket or bin, and protect the table before use.

Food Prep Area. This should be near running water, with cutting board, peeler, knives, and bowl for scraps. If you need more counter space, open a drawer and lay your cutting board across the top of it.

Bill Paying Area. If you haven't yet gone electronic, you'll just need a folder or box in which you will keep your bills, check book, envelopes, stamps and return envelopes.

Other areas to consider: A baking bin for your muffin tins, rolling pin, pastry cutter, etc. A study area for kids. A conversation area for family and friends. A play area for kids of all ages.

IT'S EASIER TO DO THE THINGS YOU NEEDTO DO WHEN THE SPACE IS READY FOR USE!

List three activity centers you will set up:

1. _____

2. _____

3. _____

Your Clothing Style

Get to know **your own clothing style** and stick to it.

When my husband got an invitation to his 40th high school reunion a few years ago, we had only been married 4 years. I was really hoping his old comrades would see me as a good choice, but I totally lost all confidence as time drew near. In desperation, I bought I a low cut top, though that is not my style, and a fancy necklace, though I don't wear jewelry. I tried them on about 300 times, spinning this way and that in front of the mirror, but they never looked right.

Then I remembered my son's kindergarten graduation party many years ago. I had my heart set on him wearing a short sleeve shirt and matching shorts with a wild animal print that I had bought on a trip to Kenya, and which had never been worn. WELL!!! Alex had other thoughts on the matter. He picked out his favorite shorts and shirt. I don't remember which ones they were, but they were not fancy. Then he **begged** me to let him wear them – and not to make him wear the "scratchy stupid" Kenya clothes. I reminded myself that it was HIS day, not mine. So why not let him wear what he wanted? So I agreed. Boy, did I learn something! When we arrived at the school, most of the kids were squirming and tugging at their brand new clothes, feet jammed into stiff new shoes. Some of the boys were even wearing neckties on that very warm day! But Alex was at ease and cheerful in his favorite comfortable clothes and thoroughly enjoyed himself.

As the reunion approached, I thought back to that day, and I returned the top and necklace to the store. In the end, I confidently wore my very favorite blouse and pants to the reunion. My only adornments were a proud husband on my arm and a happy smile on my face.

Comfort is a must, fashion is a maybe.

Planning Your Wardrobe

Once you know your clothing style, the next step is to decide *how much* and *how many* you need.

Be realistic! Consider your *current* lifestyle!

I know a woman who wears a business suit to work every day. She owns eight of them, and rotates them. No guesswork or fuss. She just wears the next one in line, and sends them to the cleaners on a regular basis. It was almost as simple as those underpants I wore in the 60's embroidered with the days of the week on them. (By the way, I once had an urge to create a line of lingerie embroidered with "Grumpy," "Foxy", "Bloated," "Frisky," "Bitchy," etc. but I didn't pursue it.)

First decide how many of each item it **makes sense** for you to own and note it in the table below, then count how many items you actually have. The difference between what you need and what you have will make it easier to let go of. Check with friends first, then consider a consignment shop for the nicer things. Then donate the rest to a thrift shop or clothing drive.

TAKE THE CHALLENGE:

Item	# Needed	# On Hand	# to Purge	Done √
Sweaters				
Shirts				
Dresses				
Tees				
Sweats				
Hoodies				
Skirts				
PJ's				
Shorts				

Your closet should only contain clothing you love to wear!

You and Your Papers

Whenever people contact me about getting organized, no matter how they present their situation ("My closets are too full," "I can't find a place for my scrapbooking materials," "I'm late for work all the time") I know there's a 95% chance that they also have some piles of unsorted, unread, uncontrolled papers lurking around. Papers seem to be one of the biggest organizing challenges we have. Here are some theories why:

Papers don't take up much space. If you have 25 books or lamp shades, they take up a lot of room and require attention. Papers quietly pile up in a corner until you suddenly have a zillion.

Papers represent unfinished business. Ugh! Worse than an unmade bed you can tackle in 5 minutes, a pile of papers may contain unpaid bills, unread articles, owner's manuals, recipes, coupons, invitations, phone numbers or addresses, business cards, etc. Each paper requires decisions and some sort of action, even if it's just filing or shredding.

Papers often arrive in our homes uninvited, through the mail, as newspapers and magazines, handouts and flyers, inserts and owner's manuals, receipts and coupons. People often feel powerless to stop the inward flow of papers because they don't know how.

There is no designated place in the home for handling papers so they tend to pile up in every room.

People are unsure which papers they need and how long to keep them. In the end, people often feel such frustration and defeat that they can actually stop dead in their tracks – like a deer in the headlights – while the papers just keep coming in.

But like handling any other project, getting a grip on your papers can be accomplished quite easily by breaking the task down into smaller steps.

Steps and Strategies for Handling Papers

- **Stop the influx** of papers. Get off generalized mailing lists by logging onto www.dmachoice.org to have your name removed. To reduce the number of catalogs you receive, log onto www.catalogchoice.org.
- **Go electronic** for bank statements, bills, recipes, owner's manuals, maps, and magazine articles.
- **Schedule daily time** to handle incoming papers and tackle backlog.
- Sort the daily mail directly into **recycle bin** or **shredder**.
- Get the **proper equipment** – file cabinet, dividers, storage boxes, stacking bins for current projects, and a rolodex for business cards.
- Work on only **one paper**/pile/project at a time to help develop better focus. In each case, choose the action that needs to be taken - to file, to read, to call, or to pay, and act accordingly. For a large sorting project, stack papers by those same action verbs for faster handling later.
- Create a "**Tickler File**" to keep items that are pending until the day you need them – the address for an upcoming seminar, your copy of a rebate form, outstanding mail orders, the lab request form for a scheduled procedure, etc.
- Create a "**To Be Logged**" folder to put addresses, phone numbers, e-mail addresses, web-sites and other notes until you have time to log them officially into a data base, phone book, calendar, etc.
- Make a **"Current Tax"** file to keep documents together till tax season.
- Make a list of **important documents** and where the original is kept (will, insurance policies, account numbers, etc.). You should update this list and share it regularly with a trusted family member or friend.
- Create a **portable reading file** you can take with you when you're traveling, sitting in a waiting room, or when you'll be stuck in traffic.
- Create a simple **file index** indicating what you've put in drawer or box.
- Put **discard dates** on boxes and files so you know when to shred them.
- **Purge regularly**, at least once a year.
- **Watch for community shredding events** to save shredding time and wear and tear on your shredder.

Landing/Launching Pad

Nothing is more annoying than having to hunt for your car keys or cell phone when it's time to leave the house!

One solution is to eliminating the problem of misplaced items is to create a "landing pad" in a practical place in your house – typically near the door- for putting your handbag, wallet, sunglasses, keys, cell phone, chewing gum, ipod, and so on THE MINUTE YOU WALK INTO THE HOUSE. It's also the "launching pad "where you know the items will be when it's time to leave for work.

The launching pad is also the perfect place to put rental items, purchases, and library books that need to be returned, your reusable shopping bags, outgoing mail, toner cartridges to recycle, and anything that belongs in the car.

Make it a GOOD habit to scoop everything up off the launching pad to take with you each time you go out the door.

List three things you should keep on your landing/launching pad:

1. _____ 2. _____ 3. _____

Quick and Easy Space Management

- Divide and conquer! Use small labeled bins and baskets to separate contents of drawers, shelves and cabinets so it's easier to find them. Think silverware divider.

- When planning meals, always "shop" first in your own pantry before heading for the grocery store. Check out on-line meal planning recipe websites and purge your old recipe/book collection.

- Create a personal basket for each family member's toiletries which they keep in their bedrooms between visits to the bathroom.

- Keep large board games under the sofa in the family room for easy reach, and save lots of shelf space.

- Use a greeting card organizer with monthly pockets to keep track of special dates and cards until you need them.

- Purge expired drug products, and divide the rest into small bins by type: "itch," "sneeze," "Rx," and "other."

- Cut back on cleaning products! Have one each for 1) hard surfaces, 2) wood, 3) windows, 4) floors, 5) sinks and toilets.

- Avoid the "collection" trap. Only buy and keep things that give you continual pleasure. Donate the rest.

- Set a timer and spend 10 minutes per day tidying up cabinets and closets. You'll reap the benefits forever.

- Save space with reusable shopping bags. Hang them on the door knob so you'll put them back into your car.

- Use a free-standing mug holder for hanging your necklaces and chains to keep them tangle-free and visible. Rings and earrings can be stored in stackable ice cube trays.

- Can't resist those hotel toiletries? Put unopened ones into a nice basket as a welcome gift for overnight guests.

Make Your Bed in the Morning

Your bed represents about a 35-square foot visual example of how good it feels when things look the way they should!

Starting your day by making your bed sets a positive standard for your day and gets you off to a good start. A nicely made bed is also very welcoming when you retire for the night.

Make your bed every day for one week.

Monday ☐

Tuesday ☐

Wednesday ☐

Thursday ☐

Friday ☐

Saturday ☐

Sunday ☐

How did that make you feel? _____

Are you ready to make that a new habit? _____

Raise Your Standards and Lower Your Expectations

A great philosophy for improving your life is to:

> ## RAISE YOUR STANDARDS
> ## AND
> ## LOWER YOUR EXPECTATIONS

Raising your standards and keeping them high is a great idea for improving your life. Aim for that perfect al dente pasta! Wear the most flattering outfit you can. Keep your plants watered just enough and rotate them each week for even sun exposure. Shop for big bargains, and so on.

What about lowering your expectations? Well, in real life, all kinds of obstacles, set-backs and road blocks can pop up at that might keep us from attaining our ideal goals. After an interruption or setback, the key to well-being is to shrug it off, bounce back, and move on.

Have standards as hard as steel
But expectations as resilient as a spring!

Aim for success but accept what comes.

Before and After Photos

Nothing motivates as naturally as success!

Taking before and after photographs of your projects is a terrific way to remind yourself of the progress you have made and to encourage you to keep on going!

Before

After

Chapter Four - Tackling Your Time

Your Most Valuable Resource

Of the personal resources that make up our lives
(time, space, energy and money),
time is the one that cannot be
renewed, repaid, reused, or reinvested.

Each day is a one-time shot, and once it's gone,
it's gone forever.

So each day we must make time to focus on
what's **most important to us**,
and strive to **make things happen**
that will **simplify and improve** our lives.

Time Management Mission Statement

Time Management Mission

**Each day, I will set aside time
to do things that truly
add value to my life,**

Avoid doing things that don't,

**And develop the ability
to know the difference.**

Jot down below five things that truly matter to you

(people, hobbies, values, goals, projects…)

1. _____

2. _____

3. _____

4. _____

5. _____

Do you devote enough time to them?

Procrastination

Procrastination is probably the **biggest obstacle** to effective time management.

If you're like most people, you would tend to put things off:

•When you don't know what to do (your computer is slow and you don't know if you should try to fix it yourself);

•When you're unsure how long the job will take or how complicated it might be (you'd like to rip out that ugly flower bed in the back yard and plant shrubs instead);

•When you're afraid of failure (you want to redo your filing system, but what if it just makes things worse?).

What can you do?

Compare risk and reward. What is the worst thing that could happen if you tackled the task today? Setting a plan, getting more information, asking friends for input – none of these will cost you anything, but may clear up some of your doubts and fears. You can also make the job less intimidating by breaking it down into smaller manageable steps. Don't be afraid to ask for help from friends or family who are on your side.

Once you've got some sort of a plan in place, set your timer for a short session, then just **plunge right in and get** started. Stay focused till the timer goes off. Be sure to leave **clean up time** at the end of the session, so you won't leave a mess and can appreciate your accomplishments!

The pain of doing a task is often less than
the painful consequences of not doing it
or the pain of lying in bed at night worrying about it!

Doing it **NOW** is much wiser than doing it *later*

Each day you put something off,
it grows bigger and bigger,
taking up more and more space
in your mind
and draining your energy.

Once you tackle that chore
you've been putting off,
you release its hold on you.
It shrinks down to its normal size
and you will regain your peace of mind.

List three things you've been putting off
and when you will get started on them:

1. _____

2. _____

3. _____

Multi-Tasking

Until quite recently, **multi-tasking** was considered a good idea **to save time**, but there are some new thoughts on the subject.

Roger Brown in InfoQ, lists some of the **dangers of multi-tasking**:

"There is evidence that multitasking actually degrades short term memory, not just for the topics being multitasked but possibly by impacting areas of the brain. Multitasking creates stress; Stress invokes the more primitive parts of the brain that are concerned with personal safety, pulling energy from the more modern parts concerned with higher level thinking. Stress can also damage cells needed for new memories.

We are more prone to errors when we multitask so the quality of our work results goes down. This, of course, adds costs to a project because things need to be fixed.

Some parts of the brain are sequential processors, able to accept only one input at a time.

The prefrontal cortex, the part of the brain most used for complex cognition and decision making, is the biggest energy consumer in the brain. Additional load from multitasking will lead to a quicker depletion of cognitive ability and more frequent need for recovery time."

If multi-tasking is counter-productive, what can we do to keep up when we have so much to do and so little time to do it?

Why not try this technique...

Double-Team Your Time

You can kill two birds with one stone
AND still keep your sanity...

By using your *brain* for one thing
While you use your *body* for another!

Your Brain	*Your Body*
Listen to an audio book	Driving your car
Phone a friend	Sewing on a button
Watch an old movie	Doing some ironing
Chat with your hubby	Enjoying a drink
Listen to nice music	Taking a brisk walk
Get cooking tips on TV	Folding the laundry

List below what you can double-team in your daily life!

Your Brain	*Your Body*

These winning combinations will not drain your brain!

Schedule Time for the Things That Matter to You

If not, they might not happen at all

8:00-9:00	Meeting on next year's budget
9:00-10:00	Budget planning
11:00-12:00	Monthly report
12:00-12:30	Lunch
12:30-1:00	Walk with coworkers
1:00-2:00	Conference call
2:00-5:00	Finalize quarterly projects

****

6:00-7:00	Dinner with family
7:00-8:00	Work on garage
8:00-9:00	Time with family
9:00-10:30	My time (bubble bath, relax)

It's your turn now. Get out your day planner and schedule time for the things that matter to you.

What have you scheduled? _____

_____

Scheduling Down Time

Says Richard Carlson, Ph.D. in **Don't Sweat the Small Stuff**:

"I've been working in the stress management field for well over a decade. In that time I've met some extraordinary people. I can't think of a single person whom I would consider to be inwardly peaceful who doesn't carve out at least a little quiet time, virtually every day. Whether it's ten minutes of meditation or yoga, spending a little time in nature, or locking the bathroom door and taking a ten-minute bath, quiet time to yourself is a vital part of life. Like spending time alone, it helps to balance the noise and confusion that infiltrate much of our day."

Use your pause button to help you find time to relax, rebalance, recharge, rewind, and rejuvenate.

What do you do to unwind?

1. _____

2. _____

3. _____

"For fast-acting relief, try slowing down."

-Lily Tomlin

The 40-Yard Dash

Like most people, you may sometimes find yourself "waking up" at some point during the day and realizing that you have zoned out and lost track of time. Perhaps you turned on the TV to see the weather forecast, and got sucked into a Jeopardy marathon that lasted most of the afternoon.

Or perhaps you started cleaning out your closet and got side-tracked by a sweat shirt belonging to a friend, which led to a phone call, then a coffee date, then OOPS! There went your day!

Well, all hope is not lost. It's time to boogie! Grab a glass of cool water, roll up your sleeves, and get caught up on your project by working faster. This doesn't mean working harder or sloppier, but in "ramming speed".

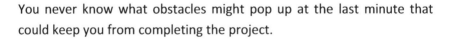

The 40-yard dash can really help you get caught up, but this technique should be used sparingly.

You never know what obstacles might pop up at the last minute that could keep you from completing the project.

Haste doesn't always make waste. It depends on how careful you are.

The Power of Ten Minutes

Some people get stuck – like a bear in a trap – when they think they don't have enough time to get much done, so they **do nothing at all**. Well, you may not have a whole day or even an hour at your disposal...

But everyone can find ten minutes!

1. Contact an old friend and make plans to meet
2. Clean out your handbag or wallet
3. Balance your checkbook
4. Plan your dinner menu
5. Prepare a shopping list using your coupons
6. Dust a room
7. Sew on a button
8. Work on your email in-bin
9. Do a few stretching exercises
10. Have a healthy snack

Don't let what you can't do right now
stop you from doing what you can do!

Time Clutter

People say time is money. But time is everything because what you can do with time is what life's all about. Break your life down and it will consist of days, weeks, school years, months, or chapters - all units of time.

Nowadays many magazine articles, books, and TV shows are devoted to the issue of household clutter which is defined as things that generate no benefit to the owner - things that are neither useful, beautiful, nor sentimental.

Well, time clutter is also a big issue in our lives. Time clutter can be defined as any activity we engage in that provides us with no memories, enhancements, connections, joy or even real relaxation.

What about TV time? Watching TV can be considered clutter time if the viewer is mindlessly channel surfing. But watching an educational show with the kids and then discussing it with them can be extremely rewarding. Cuddling up with hubby to watch an old black and white movie can be a rather romantic date night. Learning Spanish, gardening or cooking through TV is great. Whether an activity is time clutter or not depends on **purpose, balance and appreciation**.

Time = Life, Therefore, waste your time and waste your life, or master your time and master your life.   -Alan Lakein

---

What do you do that clutters your time?

1._____ 2._____ 3._____

Speed Limit

As we are speeding through our busy lives, how the heck could we possibly stop to smell a rose without getting a thorn in our nose?

As a kid, I learned a really neat trick. When I was served food I didn't like (oh, and that list was long!) I would gobble it down to get it out of the way. Then I could take my sweet time to savor the flavors of the foods I enjoyed, and leave the table with a pleasant taste in my mouth.*

We can use that same approach in life. Why don't we dash through chores we dislike - such as ironing or weeding - to leave more time to relax and enjoy pleasant past times such as a walking a park, chatting with a friend, or playing games with the kids?

A Time Trade Off Challenge	
FIND WAYS TO	
Spend Less Time	Spend More Time
Getting ready for work	Sleeping 10 more minutes
Cleaning up the kitchen	Playing Scrabble w/family
Dealing with mail	Listening to mood music

What are some chores you could speed up?

1. _____

2. _____

3. _____

*This strategy sometimes backfired when we were invited to someone's home and the attentive hostess would insist on giving me unrequested seconds because of my perceived enthusiasm. -BWG

Simple Tips for Speedy Results in your Busy Morning

90 Seconds to Make Your Bed

Lie in the middle of your bed, under the covers, and spread your arms and legs as if you are making a snow angel. Pull the sheet and blanket up and smooth them out. Then carefully fold back the covers back and slide out of bed. Fluff up the pillows, pull the covers over them and walk away with a smile. It's a great way to start the day!

90 Seconds to a Healthy Breakfast

Open fridge and take out one egg and low-fat margarine. Put one slice of whole wheat bread into toaster.

Crack an egg into microwave safe bowl and gently pierce the yolk once with a fork. Cover the bowl with a microwave safe plate and microwave it on high for 35 seconds (depending on your model). Meanwhile, butter the toast which should be done by now.

DING! Remove the "poached" egg and enjoy it with hot toast. Yummy

90 Seconds to a Bright and Sparkling Bathroom

Take glass cleaner and a paper towel from under the sink. Spray the mirror, sink, and countertop. Spray the inside of the toilet lid, the top of the seat, then open the seat and spray under the seat and around the bowl.

Take the paper towel and wipe off the mirror, the counter-top, the sink, and then the toilet in the same order as it was sprayed. Discard the paper towel, and swish the toilet bowl with a toilet brush, then flush.

Voila! Good enough until you have time for a good thorough clean.

Time Savings

The tips in this chapter can save you 18 minutes a day:

You can save 4 minutes by double teaming,
4 minutes by focusing on the job at hand,
5 minutes by preparing the night before,
and 5 minutes by speeding up daily chores.

THAT MEANS YOU WILL BE SAVING...

18 minutes per day

X 7 days a week

126 minutes per week

X 4 weeks a month

504 minutes per month

X 12 months a year

6,048 minutes per year

÷60 minutes per hour

100.8 hours of time saved

÷24 hours per day

4.2 days a year

You could take four **3-day weekends** each year with the time you saved by USING YOUR TIME MORE WISELY!

Save Time in the Morning

Create and post a checklist for morning activities so that family members can keep themselves on target.

Post a bathroom schedule on the bathroom door to avoid bottlenecks.

Pick out everyone's clothes out the night before.

Create a fool-proof "fall back" outfit for yourself and for each family member in case of a last-minute mishap.

Keep cut up fruit on hand to add to hot or cold cereal or yoghurt.

Prepare lunches ahead of time.

Freeze a couple of peanut butter and jelly sandwiches for emergencies.

Keep a jar of change near the back door.

Keep one notepad, day planner, pen, cell phone, and keys in your handbag at all times or on the launching pad.

> *Leaving for work on time assures*
> *a more relaxing drive,*
> *a punctual arrival,*
> *and a stress free start of your day.*

List 3 three things you can do to save time in the morning

1. _____

2. _____

3. _____

Keep Your Work Space Clear

Keeping your work space clear can help you clear your mind and focus on the tasks at hand.

- Don't keep a big messy pen holder on your desk when one pen will do.

- Create a trust-worthy filing system to keep track of papers and projects. Choose logical categories, and file regularly.

- Keep rarely used accessories such as tape dispenser, stapler, ruler, and hole-punch handy but not on the desk-top.

- Keep no more than two visuals (calendar or photos) on your desk at a time to prevent visual overload.

- Take the work space clutter test by seeing how long it takes you to dust it! Aim for 60 seconds or less!

> *Over 40 minutes are lost each day by executives looking for lost documents. Be smarter than they are, and PAY ATTENTION to your files!*

Note: at the end of the day, be sure to tidy up your desk, and jot down what needs to be done the next day. That makes it much easier to get off to a good start in the morning, with a clear desk and a clear idea of what needs to be done.

Just Say No!!!!

When you focus on the meaningful aspects of your life, and prioritize your time accordingly, it is much easier to reach your goals. For everything else, you should learn to say no.

Imagine this scenario. You want to be good mother to Betsy, your 6-year old, who has just joined a club. The club is holding a bake sale. To be a good mom, you have agreed to bake three dozen cupcakes and decorate them with the club colors.

You need to take the cupcakes to school tomorrow, but your boss surprised you this afternoon with an out-of-town visitor who needed last minute help with his reservations, so you got home from work 45 minutes late. Your 10-year old was having trouble with his homework and asked you to help him on the internet. It's now 8:45 pm and you haven't started the cupcakes. Betsy is crying because she can't find her teddy bear. You are feeling stressed and so you snap at her. It suddenly dawns on you that...

You snapped at your daughter because of the cupcakes that you wanted to make to show her that you are a good mother. Oh gosh. If you had said no to the cupcakes in the first place, you could have demonstrated that you are a good mother by **just being there** for her when she needed you.

Make sure that your time reflects your values
and your resources.
If not, JUST SAY NO!

Delegate

Delegating tasks to young family members not only helps relieve the household manager of some of the work, but also gives them an opportunity to feel a sense responsibility and to develop valuable life skills. Here's an example:

Job Description – Mom's Assistant
Amanda – Age 8

RESPONSIBILITIES:

1. Take dog for a walk

2. Put away the clean silverware

3. Clear the table

4. Fold clean socks

5. Bring in the mail

6. Clear and dust the coffee table

7. Put away all school books

8. Keep the coat closet tidy

****

When delegating a task for the first time, take time to explain the purpose of the task, show (not tell) how it should be done, and put in writing the deadline for completion.

> Throughout our lives, we are often valued by
> what we know how to do. Help share skills!

Don't Reinvent the Wheel

Whenever you are faced with a detailed task that is regularly repeated, such as shopping, packing for a trip, or setting up some electronic equipment, consider making yourself a customized checklist that you can use over and over again! Some of the many benefits of using a checklist include:

- The project is broken down for you into small, manageable steps.

- You don't need to rely on your memory.

- It eliminates guesswork.

- It presents steps in the most efficient order.

- It makes it easy for you to start back up at the right place after an interruption.

A checklist reduces stress and saves valuable time!

Shopping List
• **Milk/juice/coffee/tea**
• **Yoghurt/cheese/cottage cheese**
• **Bread/muffins**
• **Cereal/oatmeal/cereal bars**
• **Nuts/crackers/snacks**
• **Pudding/jello**
• **Soup**
• **Fresh/canned fruit**
• **Fresh/frozen vegetables**
• **Condiments**
• **Shampoo/cream/soap/dental**
• **Prescriptions**
• **Dietary supplements**
• **Paper products**
• **Cleaning products**

List some of your tasks that would be easier with a checklist:

1._____ 2._____ 3._____

Chapter Five - Harnessing Your Energy

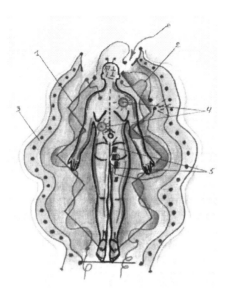

Your Most Vital Resource

We each only have so much energy each day.

So we must try to find moments in the day

When we can unwind and reset our energy levels

to the fresh, vibrant feeling

of having just stepped out of a perfect shower.

> **"The energy of the mind is the essence of life."**
> **-Aristotle**

Play

"A physical or mental leisure activity that is undertaken purely for enjoyment or amusement and has no other objective."

Kids love to...

Play in the street
Play in the park
Play in the tree house
And play after the dark

Play with their hands
Play with their toys
Play with their pals
And make lots of noise

Play with their thoughts
or play with some string -
Kids have the skill
To play anything.

"The creation of something new is not accomplished by the intellect but by the play instinct."   -Carl Jung

The Power of Sleep

"Many of us want to sleep as little as possible—or feel like we have to. There are so many things that seem more interesting or important than getting a few more hours of sleep.

But just as exercise and nutrition are essential for optimal health and happiness, so is sleep. The quality of your sleep directly affects the quality of your waking life, including your mental sharpness, productivity, emotional balance, creativity, physical vitality, and even your weight.

No other activity delivers so many benefits with so little effort! "

http://helpguide.org/life/sleeping.htm

> Blessed is the person who is too busy to worry in the daytime and too sleepy to worry at night.
>
> -anon

According to the Mayo Clinic, here are seven simple things you can do to improve your sleep:

1. Stick to a sleep schedule (including weekends)
2. Pay attention to what you eat and drink (caffeine, alcohol)
3. Create a bedtime ritual (relax with a bath, book, music)
4. Get comfortable (temperature, light, sound, bedding)
5. Limit daytime naps
6. Include physical activity early in your daily routine
7. Manage stress

Record your bedtime for the next five nights. How regular is it?
1._____ 2._____ 3._____ 4._____ 5._____

Watch Out for Worry

The preacher looked out over the congregation, and solemnly stated "Watch out for worrying needlessly. Most of the things you worry about never happen." One parishioner in the back row loudly replied, "See? It obviously works."  Unfortunately, worrying won't prevent scary things from happening.

Let's look at the difference between **worrying** (passively and negatively focusing on the worst case scenario) and **planning** (actively focusing on what to do if the worst case scenario should manifest itself). It reminds me of when my son and I lived on the 5th floor of an apartment building that had one stairwell and no fire escape. When I thought about it, I'd lie in bed and worry about what would happen if there were a fire. Eventually, I decided I'd be better off planning rather than worrying, and bought a sturdy rope ladder. No more sleepless nights. If you are stuck in fear of a catastrophe, plan ahead and take action!

When I was in my 20's, I lived in a Southern California beach town where the night life was lively. I was often invited out to dinner, but was always embarrassed to ask how to dress, because I didn't want to put my date on the spot. I devised a foolproof plan to make sure that I was never under dressed or over dressed for my date. I would have laid out three different outfits on my bed – one very casual, one semi-casual, and one more formal. When my date arrived, my room-mate would answer the door, then dash into my room and point to one of the outfits, which I'd hop into like Superwoman, and my date was never the wiser.

- Plan Purposefully
- Prepare Positively
- Proceed Powerfully
- Pursue Persistently

Develop Your Focus

Try this experiment. Take a deep breath, relax your shoulders, and look around the room. Count how many red objects you can see.

Now, without looking, try to recall how many green objects you saw. How many yellow ones? **We see what we focus on.**

- **Focus provides clarity.**
- **Focus gives us energy.**
- **Focus helps us find what we want.**

Focus is a skill you can develop. Today you may only be able to focus for ten minutes, but if you work at it, you can expand your focus to longer and longer periods. It's when we are focused that we accomplish our most important tasks, and use less energy doing it!

If you need help getting and staying focused, use a simple kitchen timer. Start by setting it for 10 minutes and stay 100% focused till it rings! No cheating! No answering your cell phone or peeking at e-mails! Each time you use it, set it for 5 minutes longer, until you have developed a functioning focus on and off switch!

Record your longest focus time:

Day 1 _____ Day 2 _____ Day 3 _____ Day 4 _____

Find yourself a carrot

When I think about motivation, I always picture a carrot. I know that if I get stuck on a project, I need to have a clear vision of what it is I will gain by moving forward with it - my own personal carrot).

When I put myself through college when I was in my 20's, it was one of the hardest things I have ever done – I had a long commute to have affordable housing, two or three part time jobs at any given time, and a heavy course load to get my degree faster. MY CARROT was the clear vision I had of getting my diploma and a chance to get a decent job.

If you would like to lose 15 pounds, save enough money to go to Cancun for a vacation, or create a craft center in a spare closet, PICTURE IT. Literally! Look through magazines to find a picture that shows a slim figure in a bathing suit, a Caribbean beach resort, the perfect craft center. Cut it out and post it where you can see it. This will help keep you motivated to achieve your dream!

It is a terrible thing to see and have no vision.
-Helen Keller

Your Relationships

Your spouse

Your neighbor

Your coworker

Your best friend

Your kids

Your bridge partner

YOUR BOSS

Your nephew

Your grandchild

Your teammate

A relationship is

1. The state of being **connected** or **related**

2. An **association** by blood or marriage; kinship

3. The **mutual** dealings, **connections**, or feelings that exist between two parties, countries, people, etc.

> You don't **own** any other creature on this planet. Not your husband, your wife, your children, your parents. All you own is **your half of your relationship** with them. How can you enhance that relationship?
>
> -Unknown

If you make people and relationships your hobby, you will never be short of supplies. As Barbra Streisand sang, "People who need people are the luckiest people in the world."

The Yin and Yang of Love

My husband, Bob, who had a stable middle-class upbringing in Pennsylvania, loves the somewhat mournful sound of a distant freight train, with the thud thud thud thud of the cars moving purposefully along. To him, the sound signifies freedom and adventure. He pictures the train moving towards an unknown but awesome and adventuresome destination somewhere out west.

I hate the sound of a freight train. It fills me with a feeling of being stuck, trapped, imprisoned. I grew up out west in the poor part of Phoenix, Arizona. Flat, hot, dusty, brown. Our rented house was about 40 yards from the train tracks, so I heard freight trains all day long and all night long, tooting, screeching and shuddering through my thoughts and dreams. It might have been heading for an exciting unknown adventuresome destination somewhere out west, but it would leave me where I was, with nothing but the hot creosote smell of the railroad ties and an occasional flattened penny.

So who is right? Is the hoot of the freight train pleasant or unpleasant? It's not a case of **right or wrong** but more like a case of **right or left**. It's a question of perception –how it appears from where you are standing. By the same token, my husband loves Christmas and I dread it. I like the smell of dryer sheets but he hates it. Right or left. Left or right? By the way, we can even ask if it is **your** left or **my** left?

"All married couples should learn the art of battle as they should learn the art of making love. Good battle is objective and honest - never vicious or cruel. Good battle is healthy and constructive, and brings to a marriage the principles of equal partnership. "   -Ann Landers

Forget Perfection!

In "Marry Him – A Case for Settling for Mr. Good Enough", author Lori Gottleib says that most woman start off with a real or imaginary checklist. Each time the guy in question doesn't meet the ideal, he gets points off. Doesn't like cats? Ten points off. Loves to watch Monday night football with his pals? Ten points off. Thinning a bit on top? Ten points off.

She says it should go the other way. Start at zero and build up. Has a steady job? Add ten points. Always remembers his parents' birthdays? Add ten points. Likes to cook? Add twenty points.

We can even evaluate a job that way. In the end, there are usually only three or four great things about the job that outweigh the less attractive aspects.

Think about your partner's attributes. How does he contribute to the quality of your life? _____

How about your attributes? How do you make a positive impact on your partner's life? _____

"Success in marriage does not come merely through finding the right mate, but through being the right mate."   -Barnett Brickner

---

Become an Island

Although Thomas Mann said "No man is an island unto himself," there are times when it's best for us to pull back onto a personal little island, even for a short while.

Think back to a time when you had to wear shoes that didn't fit. Too tight, too stiff, heels were too high? How did you manage to get through that wedding, graduation ceremony, funeral, whatever? I bet you had to turn off your feelings and ignore the pain.

Well, that type of pain is what we often feel when we are wearing the cloak of someone else's expectations. We have to shut ourselves off to the pain to get by, but that means we are also shutting ourselves off from life.

When we have a tough role to fulfill that doesn't fit very well, we need to have our own little mental island of peace and pleasure – a sort of recharging station, where we can go to escape from time to time. If we can create this type of island in our minds, and not depend on drugs, alcohol, video games, or shopping sprees to get that feeling of escape, then we can go to that **secret place** any time we want, with no negative ramifications.

Imagine an invisible raincoat you could drape over your shoulders when you know you have to deal with an abrasive personality, enter a room full of strangers, or give a presentation to an unknown audience. That's when your island can serve you well. It is very important that you learn to be attentive to yourself and to your need, after all -

YOUR RELATIONSHIP WITH YOURSELF is the only one you're sure to have to deal with your entire life!!!!

By the way, why does the word "selfish" have such a bad reputation? There are times when we must consider SELF before tending to others. Next time you are on a plane, preparing for take-off, listen to the flight attendant's warning: "Be sure to attach your oxygen mask first before assisting others." Why? Because you won't do anyone any good if you don't take the time to look after your own health and well being.

It is also very good for you to have a **physical place** in your home where you can go to lick your wounds, day dream, zone out and relax. You don't need to be an entire room – it may only be a favorite chair - but the important thing is that when you sit there, you feel AT HOME IN YOUR SPIRIT!

Everybody needs a personal nook where thoughts and feelings are allowed have total freedom!

"It isn't what you have, or who you are, or where you are, or what you are doing that makes you happy or unhappy. It is what you think about."
-Dale Carnegie

The Not Quite Golden Rule

Do unto others
as they would have
you do unto them.

In other words,
don't scratch someone else's back
where yours itches.

For years, I struggled to keep my husband's sock drawer and clothes closet neat and well-organized as a sign of my love for him - until he told me that we would much rather have back massage. I had fallen into the trap of scratching his back where mine itched. Lucky is the person whose partner can figure this out faster than I could!

Simple Energy-Boosting Activities

- ☐ Set a goal for the week
- ☐ Have a good laugh
- ☐ Get up and stretch
- ☐ Call an old friend
- ☐ Take a walk
- ☐ Visit someone
- ☐ Do something creative
- ☐ Tidy up a drawer or cabinet
- ☐ Have a healthy snack
- ☐ Recycle something
- ☐ Cheer someone up
- ☐ Read a good book
- ☐ Do a puzzle
- ☐ Tackle a paper or two
- ☐ Get a good night's sleep
- ☐ Count your blessings

What do you do to feel energized?
1._____ 2._____ 3._____
What could you do to help others feel energized?
1._____ 2._____ 3._____

An Attitude of Gratitude

The feeling of happiness is
like having your back scratched.
You can more fully appreciate it
when you actually have an itchy back.

Floating on a rubber raft
in a swimming pool
is relaxing and nice,
safe and comfortable.

But true happiness is
more than just comfort.
It's the rush of feeling you get
when you realize
just how relaxed,
safe and comfortable you are
compared to how you could be.
It's like coming in from the rain.

Happiness comes from
an attitude of gratitude.

Our Possessions

It's not how much we possess,

but what we truly *love*,

use and *appreciate*

that results in happiness.

"He is a wise man who does not grieve for the things which he has
not, but rejoices for those which he has."   -Epictetus

Forgive Everyone, Including YOURSELF

We are all human and that means we make mistakes. Making mistakes can be a positive sign that we are stretching ourselves and reaching outside our sphere of knowledge or experience.

Mastering the art of forgiveness – starting with forgiving ourselves – is the way to turn a mishap into a lesson, and to learn and grow from it. Forgiveness is the both the father and the child of maturity, wisdom and strength.

"To forgive is to set a prisoner free and discover that the prisoner was you."   Louis B. Smedes

"The weak can never forgive. Forgiveness is the attribute of the strong."   - Mahatma Gandhi

"Forgiveness is the key to action and freedom."
                                                        -Hannah Arendt

"It's toughest to forgive ourselves. So it's probably best to start with other people. It's almost like peeling an onion. Layer by layer, forgiving others, you really do get to the point where you can forgive yourself."   -Patty Duke

"Forgiveness does not change the past, but it does enlarge the future. "   -Paul Boese

List two acts of forgiveness that would help you move on:

1._____

2. _____

Chapter Six - Your Money

Money is a funny thing. Many people associate it with quality, value, success, and status, but in fact, it is less valuable to our overall well being than health, freedom, or quality relationships.

The concept and use of money have evolved over time. It's a fact that some people have always possessed things that others didn't have, and vice versa. Before money existed, people made direct exchanges of goods with each other to balance out their needs. This was called bartering.

According to history, around 1200 BC, shells were used in China as a unit of exchange. Later metal coins were used as units of exchange, then it evolved to pieces of colored paper.

Nowadays, exchanges are made WITHOUT MONEY EVEN CHANGING HANDS. The value of this theoretical "currency" fluctuates constantly based on who-knows-what economic theories, and these fluctuations seriously impact our busnesses, our jobs, and our budgets.

Gee – how much simpler life would be if I could just trade my carrots for your squash. Ho hum.

"The use of money is all the advantage there is in having it."
-Benjamin Franklin

The Best Things in Life Aren't Even Things

The best things in life
are relationships,
experiences,
adventures,
discoveries,
memorable vistas
celebrations,
and opportunities
to share and guide,
relax and grow
with family and friends
or even all alone.

Sleuth Your Expenses!

If you want to manage your money, you're going to have to know what comes in versus what goes out. By the way, the key is to have less going out than coming in!

Become your own money Private Eye! Track your spending for one whole month. It isn't that hard to do.

- For expenses you pay by check or bank payment, use your bank statement.
- For cash expenses, use a 3 x 5 card in your wallet. Jot down each expense.
- If you pay by credit card, use your credit card statement to track your spending.
- Record your findings on the following Budget Worksheet

THE BIG TRADE OFF
It will probably take you about ten minutes a day
for just one month – that is a total of...
Five Hours to Getting Financially Savvy.
That's a pretty good investment of your time.
You can make up that time by
simply laying out your clothes at night
and hanging up your car keys every day!

Budget Worksheet

Fill this out and see how to plan for a balanced budget. It's not rocket science!

Category	Monthly Cost
Rent/mortgage	
Heat	
Electricity/gas	
Cable/Internet	
Other utility	
Taxes not withheld	
Cell phone	
Car payments	
Car insurance	
Gas/Maintenance	
Health insurance	
Medical expenses	
Child/pet care	
Grocery/household	
Clothing	
Grooming	
Eating out	
Movies	
Magazines, books	
Gym and exercise	
Entertainment	
Misc	
Total monthly expenses	
Total take home pay	
Available balance	
Amount to save	

Do It Yourself

One of the best way to save money is NOT TO PAY SOMEONE TO DO WHAT YOU CAN DO.

Of course, doing it yourself depends on the availability of your time, energy and space.

But doing more for yourself is something to consider.

Instead of driving to Dunkin' Donuts or Starbucks for your morning java, make it yourself at home.

You can also consider doing for your own nails, your dry cleaning with a kit, and your own brown bag lunch for work.

If you get courageous, you could try cutting your own hair, at least the in-between trims!

Filtering tap water instead of purchasing water saves money and helps the environment.

You can have great fun helping your kids make their own Halloween costumes.

You could try offering some homemade cards and gifts at holiday time which will make a lasting impression.

List three things you currently do yourself:

1. _____ 2._____ 3._____

List three more things you would consider doing:

1. _____ 2._____ 3._____

Free (or Almost Free) Fun Things to Do

1. Have a pot luck dinner with friends.

2. Play hide and seek with the kids/grandkids.

3. Visit each and every park in your area.

4. Spend an evening at the public library.

5. Take a free online course.

6. Sample new recipes.

7. Make a hand-made greeting card.

8. Join a book club.

9. Wander around a college campus.

10. Have a game board evening with friends.

11. Look for free arts and craft events.

12. Walk a dog (even if it's the neighbor's).

13. Play in the sprinkler.

14. Cut up old magazines to make a vision board.

15. Try bird watching.

16. Clean out the attic and have a yard sale.

17. Put on some lively music and DANCE.

18. Do some volunteer work in your community.

19. Learn to meditate.

20. Make a snowman.

Make it Easy to be Good and Hard to be Bad with Your Money

Dare to set up your life in a brand new way.

1. Always keep cut up celery, cucumbers and carrots in the fridge for a quick snack. Cheaper and healthier than chips or crackers!
2. Set up an automatic savings program through work or your bank.
3. Keep a credit card to use for emergencies only. Wrap it in a warning note to yourself to make it hard to access. Otherwise, use a debit card and deduct each transaction as it occurs.
4. Plan your shopping so you can avoid convenience stores.
5. Bake and freeze your own healthy muffins so you have a supply on hand. Just pop one into the microwave and it will taste fresh.
6. Keep a variety of inexpensive greeting cards in your card organizer for unexpected occasions.
7. If you want to splurge on a weekly take-out, be sure to use coupons, watch for specials, and don't order beverages.
8. Keep take-out menus and coupons in a folder near the phone or in the car.
9. Buy sports drinks in powdered concentrate so you can make your own and keep a pitcher in the fridge.
10. Make a list of quick and easy meals that you can put together on busy nights, and keep your pantry and freezer stocked with the necessary ingredients.

What are your easiest meals? _____

What does your pantry need? _____

Grocery Shopping Tips

- Create your own customized **pre-printed shopping list** for shopping at your grocery store and at your super discount store. Then stick to the list!

- Shop in **your own pantry** or fridge first to use up what you have.

- **Don't shop hungry**, lonely, or angry.

- **Avoid the middle aisles**, which contain less basic items.

- **Compare coupon discounted prices** with the price of store brands to see which saves you more money.

- **Don't buy more than you can use**, even if it's free, or you will have to store it and it might expire.

- **Plan your meals** then plan your shopping, so you always have on hand what you need.

- **Serve chicken and turkey more often** than red meat. Buy whole chickens for roasting, then use the leftovers to make soup.

- **Don't assume you save by buying the larger sizes**. Read the tags to find the price per unit cost and check the lower shelves for lower prices.

- **Buy non-fat dry milk** and make it yourself. If you don't like the taste, use it for cooking or on cereal.

- **Bulk cooked cereals are much cheaper than individual packets.** Cook oatmeal using half milk and half water. Add chopped apple and a pinch of cinnamon while cooking. It's healthy and delicious!

- **Learn when your store marks their meats down**. Most places do this on the same day each week, and it means big savings for you.

- **Two for $5 equals $2.50 each**. This means you don't have to buy two to get the discounted price. When it's "buy one, get one free" some stores will give you 50% off even if you buy only one. Ask the store manager for their store policy.

- **If you shop in more than one place to save money,** be sure to economize gas by combining errands.

Solve Your Problems with Actions, not Purchases

It's wise to dream, but our dreams can often be realized better through wise actions than through reactive purchases. So put away your credit card and think.

Here are some examples. Jeanette wants more variety in her life. But instead of joining a club (where she could meet some interesting people), she subscribes to a recipe book-of-the-month club. The recipe books may make her life more interesting for an hour or two, but are not worth the cost of the books and the precious room they take up. These books will do nothing to combat her loneliness.

Miranda runs out and purchases a pretty set of stacking desk-top bins in hopes of achieving her dream of a clutter-free office. But what she really needs is to do is to purge the years of paper backlog she has, and devise a plan for how to keep the daily influx of junk mail out of her life. Stacking bins won't do that for her!

Candace dreams of getting married one day, so she subscribes to several bride and wedding magazines, convincing herself that she is taking action towards achieving her dream. The magazines don't cost a lot of money, but a better use of her resources would be to join a gym and get in shape so she can develop the confidence to go out and meet a potential boyfriend she can perhaps one day marry.

Then there's Lucille, who keeps shopping at yard sales and thrift store for her dream home – a pretty curio cabinet, painted bookshelves, an upholstered foot stool, lacey bedroom curtains, etc. The purchases were "bargains" but they won't do her any good in her tiny over-stuffed apartment. What she should be doing is setting up a savings plan so that she can one day afford to buy her own place.

> *"There are people who have money and people who are rich."*
> *-Coco Chanel*

Squirrels Collect But Don't Hoard!

It's instinctive for squirrels
to collect nuts to see them through
the long winter months.

But there is instinctive wisdom
in the quantities they amass.

You don't see them scurrying out
to buy big plastic storage bins
during the January sales!

Be as wise as a squirrel!
Collect for a purpose
but don't hoard.

On the subject of wisdom, I am still trying to understand why
we consider the owl to be so wise, when he asks the same
dumb question overe and over again? -BWG

How to Save on Electric Bills

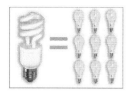

- **Switch off your computer at night**. Eliminate phantom electrical drain by switching off the power strip. Save up to $75 per year.
- **Use Energy Star appliances when possible.** They save money for the consumer and protect the environment.
- **Keep your fridge and freezer full**. Your fridge and freezer use about 1/6 of your home energy, more than any other appliance. Since solid items hold cold better than air does, less energy is used when they are full, so try filling up spaces with cans of water or ice.
- **Keep the fridge door shut.** Keep commonly used items in front. Create a "sandwich basket" for cold cuts and condiments. A pitcher of cold drinking water will keep the fridge cold and eliminates the need to run tap water till it gets cold.
- **Lighting represents 15% of your electric bill.** Use energy efficient CFL bulbs, motion-sensor and/or solar powered lights outside. At holiday time, use LED lights. *Consumer Reports says* LEDs are better for the environment; run much cooler, reducing fire risk; should last longer; and save money.
- **Line dry**. Dry your laundry outdoors until it gets too cold then use your home heat to dry your clothes in winter. This will keep your living space a bit moister, preventing colds and sinus infections.
- **Keep filters and vents clean.** That includes dryer vent, A/C and heating filters, fan blades, and oven, fridge or microwave vents. Any blockage of air creates an unnecessary energy drain.
- **Buy a programmable thermostat**. The jury is out on the efficiency of varying day and night time temperatures, but it seems wiser to let your house cool off on winter nights, then kick back up in the morning. At least it's healthier to sleep in a cool room.
- **Turn down your water heater**. Most are set at 160º, but 130º is as efficient and safer to the skin. You'll save up to $270 per year.
- **Wash your clothes in cold water**. Laundering most loads in cold water will save wear and tear on clothes, and up to $145 a year on your electric bill.

How to Save on Gas

1. **Get a smaller car**. This is a long term goal, but shop ahead so you are ready when it is time to change cars. Better gas mileage = less pollution. If yours is a multi-vehicle household, *use the smaller car* whenever you can.
2. **Use public transportation.** This is a tough task, but it's a good idea to get used to for when you can no longer drive.
3. **Keep your car well-maintained.** A car in good condition uses less oil and gas and is easier on the environment.
4. **Keep your tires inflated**. This increases gas efficiency as well as helps the tires reach their life expectancy.
5. **Combine errands**. Try to think "errands per gallon" by creating a circuit to include, for example, a visit to the bank, drug story, video store, library, paper recycling bin, and grocery store all in one shot. If the grocery store is out of the way, take a little cooler with you for refrigerated items.
6. **Slow down and even your speed**. If you drive at 65 mph instead of 80 mph you will save about 15% at the pump. Save more gas money by using your gas and brake pedals sparingly.
7. **Keep your windows closed**. It's amazing how that air flow into your vehicle pulls it back and makes the engine work harder.
8. **Use your A/C at a minimum.** How can you keep windows closed and NOT use A/C? Use your outside air vent when possible.
9. **Travel light**. Keep your trunk empty of anything heavy that you don't need. Every little pound counts!
10. **Carpool or barter for errands**. When you share the same soccer games, bake sales, and cheerleading practice as other parents, consider taking turns driving, or riding together. This helps build relationships, and can make things more fun for everyone.

Reduce, Reuse, Recycle

Help our tiny planet!

Reduce spending. Shop in your own closet, pantry, or book shelves first before heading to the store to buy more stuff. Use a list and shop wisely. If you buy something on impulse, you can probably return it for a full refund. Decrease expenses by increasing your insurance deductibles, and get rid of your land phone if you have a cell phone.

Reuse whenever possible. There are lots of ways to reuse. A broach can be clipped onto a chain as a pretty pendant. A vase can be used to hold kitchen utensils. An old pillow case makes a handy laundry bag or garment cover. Rubber bands make great grippers on hangers and jar lids. Be creative!

Shop second hand. Buying used not only saves money on your purchases, but is a kind of reusing. Instead of buying new books, DVD's, CD's, and magazines, use the resources available at the public library..

Recycle. When you have items you no longer need, sell them on eBay or consignment, give them to a friend or family member, donate them to a charity, or as a last result, take them to a recycle center. Throwing things away is the last resort, because THERE IS NO SUCH THING AS *"AWAY."* Anything you throw away will still be on our planet for about another 4 million years.

Refuse. Buck the system when you can. Take your own bags to the grocery store and refuse a bag whenever possible. Get off the junk mailing lists to reduce incoming mail. Stop subscribing to magazines, buying every new gadget under the sun, refuse "free items" that will just cause you space problems or exorbitant shipping and handling costs.

What are some ways you could cut back your consumption?

How to Have a Great Yard Sale

Not all yard sales are created equal. In some cases, folks drive right by with hardly a sideways glance, while others attract crowds like ants at a picnic. Much of the attraction depends on how well you've set it up.

Planning
Ask yourself honestly if having a yard sale is for you. Recruit help for the project from family members, neighbors, or friends. Choose a date that suits everyone, with a back-up rain date. Plan what to do with things that don't sell during the yard sale, such take them to a thrift shop.

Preparation
Get a permit from the local authorities (if needed). Place an ad in the local newspaper. Make up signs for busy street corners, before each major turn.

Gather up little round price stickers, baggies, marking pens, plastic shopping bags, and tables for displaying.

Get plenty of change and a pouch or bag to hold the money. Then get everything ready - clean and price each item as you go along. It's a good idea to make grab bags of smaller items such as buttons, pencils, pens or tiny toys.

Make signs such as "All Baskets $1" or "All Paperback Books 25¢." Assign tasks (cashier, packer) and decide if prices will be negotiable.

Presentation
Use a variety of tables, benches, or shelves and display items by category, such as bath, kitchen, games, etc. Keep smiling! A friendly atmosphere promotes spending! Rearrange displays to keep them full and keep items visible. Near wind-up time, lower prices, or try "buy one, get one free."

Wind Up
Load leftovers into vehicles and drop them off for donation. Celebrate!

Chapter Six - Follow Through

Now that you have a good idea of what it takes to achieve a simpler, well-balanced life, the key to getting there is to follow through.

"You have to have confidence in your ability, and then be tough enough to follow through."   -Rosalynn Carter

"Do not dwell in the past, do not dream of the future, concentrate the mind on the present moment."

-Buddha

"I can give you a six-word formula for success: Think things through, then follow through."

-Sir Walter Scott

"You can't build a reputation on what you are going to do."

– Henry Ford

"Many of life's failures are people who did not realize how close they were to success when they gave up."   – Thomas Edison

A Well Balanced Life

We all seem to struggle with trying to make sure to take care of priorities, not overlook the basics, and maintain a balanced life.

One way to achieve this is to use a weekly top priority to-do list that includes all important areas of your life.

Here is a sample of a weekly plan which you could customize with specific categories that represent your needs. The plan is intended to include only items you plan to do **this week**. Anything not intended for this week should be noted elsewhere. The reason many to-do lists fail is that they become mental dumping grounds for all sorts of tasks and don't reflect a realistic plan. Keep this realistic!

Note: for everyone, your health should be category #1!

Health	Job	Finances
·Gym Tues/Thurs ·Schedule doctor	·Boss's birthday ·9 am meeting Mon	·Start taxes ·Call insurance ·Balance checkbook
Social ·Call Sue Monday ·Bridge Weds	**Home Projects** ·LR curtains ·Call plumber ·Hang new print	**Pets & Plants** ·Replant ficus ·Cat to vet ·Order mulch
Hobbies ·Sort photos ·Plan vacation ·Order patterns	**Family** ·Jeff soccer Monday ·Meg dentist? ·Frank in NYC	**Special** ·Car inspection ·Research tire prices

Your Ripple Effect

Each of us has a ripple effect,

even though it may not be visible now.

Do what you can do to make sure

that the ripples you create

reflect your deepest values

and your highest aspirations.

This is how a culture is formed -

one small drop at a time.

List three people who are affected by your words and actions.

1._____ 2._____ 3._____

If at First You Don't Succeed, Tweak Tweak Tweak!

 According to Jim Clemmer in "Growing the Distance: Timeless Principles for Personal, Career, and Family Success" -

"In 1914 Thomas Edison's factory in West Orange, New Jersey, was virtually destroyed by fire. Although the damage exceeded $2 million, the buildings were insured for only $238,000 because they were made of concrete and were thought to be fireproof. Much of Edison's life work went up in smoke and flames that December night. At the height of the fire, Edison's 24-year-old son, Charles, searched frantically for his father. He finally found him, calmly watching the fire, his face glowing in the reflection, his white hair blowing in the wind.

'My heart ached for him,' said Charles. 'He was 67 — no longer a young man — and everything was going up in flames. When he saw me, he shouted, "Charles, where's your mother?" When I told him I didn't know, he said, "Find her. Bring her here. She will never see anything like this as long as she lives."'

The next morning, Edison looked at the ruins and said, 'There is great value in disaster. All our mistakes are burned up. Thank God we can start anew.'

Three weeks after the fire, Edison managed to deliver the first phonograph."

By the way, Edison was attributed with 10,000 failed attempts at the light bulb before he got it right. So why should we criticize ourselves if we are not YET able to manage our STEAM? Try *something*, and tweak it. If it doesn't work, tweak it again!

List something you need to tweak: _____

94

The Cycle of Growth

$$\begin{array}{ccc}
 & \text{Believe} & \\
 \nearrow & & \searrow \\
 \text{Conceive} & \leftarrow & \text{Achieve}
\end{array}$$

This cycle of growth consists of first conceiving a dream, then believing that it is possible, and finally achieving and living that dream.

Following this cycle will help you continue to grow throughout your lifetime.

Just remember to realize where you are each step of the way, and be sure to enjoy the journey.

We too often limit our belief in our own capabilities and those low limits can become a self-fulfilling prophesy. If, for example, you believe you are a poor student, you'll probably be uncomfortable in any learning environment. That discomfort might block you from participating well in a class, and inhibit your performance on a test, resulting in a lower grade than you deserve! ***Believe Yourself to Be a Winner!!***

"Though no one can go back and make a brand new start, anyone can start from now and make a brand new ending."   – Anonymous

Create Your Own Milestones

When we are kids, things happen to us – bad things like when a pet dies, a best friend moves away, or a bike gets stolen. Good things happen to us, too, like having a really nice 5th grade teacher, getting a new pair of roller skates, getting an opportunity to learn to swim. Then one day, we realize that we can **make** things happen - good things - important things - and that we don't have to just sit and wait for things to happen to us. Making things happen are what I call home-made milestones.

Some of my home-made milestones included moving out of hot boring Phoenix to live in fun cool Hermosa Beach, California when I was 22 years old. Another milestone was deciding at 23 to go back to college to get my degree. Another was becoming a seamstress at age 26. Yet another was becoming an ESL teacher in Switzerland at age 28.

How did I have the guts to make these big moves from state to state, country to country? Well, a long time ago, I consulted a wise, philosophical man about a decision I was having trouble making and I explained in detail my alternatives. He listened and responded, but did not choose the path for me. Instead he asked, "Do you know how to be sure that you are making the right decision?" I held my breath in anticipation of the answer. He said, "When you make it right." He let me think about it for a minute. "You see," he continued, "we can never be sure what lies in the road ahead. But once we chose a path, we must be **fully committed to making it work by whatever means it takes**. And then it will become the right decision. No looking back. No regrets. Just keep moving forward."

And there were situations to come in my life when I had to remind myself of his words, when I'd find myself saying, "Oh, dear, what kind of a mess have I got myself into THIS time?" such as when I once found myself stuck on a roof trying to replace a cap on an exhaust vent, or when I spent my first two hours in London in jail, or when I slept in the back seat of a car on a back street in Paris. I can think back and smile at these memories now, but at the time, I was just plain scared. Somehow I always manage to find a way out and to move forward.

As Frankie would sign, "I just pick myself up and get back in the race."

My very favorite movie is about a guy who has to pick himself up every day and take a new shot at it. Over and over, day after day, misanthrope Bill Murray screws up royally, with botched suicides, outrageously inappropriate behavior, and failed attempts at courtship. But by golly, he finally does get it right. It's a treat to see the positive ripple effects he makes on the wonderful people participating in his final perfect version of Groundhog Day.

One thing we know for sure about life is that change is inevitable. The trick is to catch its wind and adjust our sails so that it may take us in the direction we truly want to go.

As you explore new ways to manage your Space, Time, Energy and Money, don't be afraid to fail. It's not a four-letter word. It's just life showing you may not quite have it right yet. Be an Edison! Never give up till the light bulb goes off!

I wish you the best of luck – but more importantly – I wish you the power to believe that you can, with a combination of will and skill, achieve the simple, well-balanced life you deserve.

Bev

"Simplicity is the ultimate sophistication."   -Leonardo da Vinci

Made in the USA
Charleston, SC
16 March 2012